"These are beautiful and terrifying prayers, part praise, part lament, all radically God-centered. Written with a clear-eyed view of death's approach, they trace the geography of pain in a body that is no longer healthy and a spirit battered in the struggle for meaning. Fragments of the Hebrew psalms weave through these passionate, faith-filled outpourings, with the uncanny result that they sound as old and familiar as the Bible and as new as today's troubles. These psalms will be immensely helpful to people in affliction, for out of the depths they witness to the only hope that can help: even in darkness, God's gracious presence is here to redeem."

Elizabeth Johnson, C.S.J.
Professor of Theology, Fordham University

"In his extraordinary psalms John Carmody raises some of the hardest questions of Christian faith, including one every devotional poet must struggle with: 'What is our song to be?' These wonderful and agonizing poems are his answer to that question, and what a ringing answer it is, as human as the telephone call to a close friend, as awestruck as the gaze of the suppliant confronted with the unfathomable mystery of God."

Alfred Corn

"These are the psalms of a poet who wrestles with God and comes away with a blessing. No easy consolation is offered in these pages. Instead, individual troubles are faced squarely in their pain and terror, and placed with hard-won hope in the wider context of human suffering and the mystery of God's care. One can pray these psalms and experience the grace of connection, endurance, and trust without pretending the pain makes sense by any human standards."

Anne E. Patrick, S.N.J.M.
Professor of Religion, Carleton College

PSALMS
for times of trouble

JOHN CARMODY

TWENTY-THIRD PUBLICATIONS
Mystic, CT 06355

Twenty-Third Publications
185 Willow Street
P.O. Box 180
Mystic, CT 06355
(203) 536-2611
800-321-0411

ISBN 0-89622-614-X
Library of Congress Catalog Card Number 94-60847
Printed in the U.S.A.

For Leo O'Donovan, S.J.

CONTENTS

INTRODUCTION

This is a book of prayers. Most of them try to make the mood of the moment, the prevailing spiritual passion, into a claim upon God. Obviously, the great model I have in mind is the Book of Psalms that one finds in the Bible.

God, Psalms, and Prayer

Traditionally, King David is credited with having composed the biblical psalms, though few historical or literary critics would subscribe to that opinion nowadays. In writing these prayers, I have sometimes imagined David working at his lyre. It has been a consoling image, because the King was no immaculate believer. His great virtue was the ardor of his faith, which the biblical judges of such matters apparently found to cover a multitude of sins: murder, adultery, duplicity. How much did those judges forgive him because he sang his prayers well? How much can we hope to avoid, be forgiven, if we can find in our hearts, our souls, images worthy of the beauty of God?

The psalms are personal, of course, addressed to a God presumed to take an interest in our lives, maintain a stake in our fortunes. The background is the covenant that biblical believers (Jews, Christians, and Muslims alike) have thought the Creator struck with them: choosing them to be God's people, with whom God would sojourn, through good times and bad. Because of this covenant, this common life, singers of psalms can lift their voices toward God as toward a friend, an intimate, a lover.

Certainly, God remains "the Lord," sovereign in all ways. Nonetheless, God is also "our Lord," a divinity we can imagine holding shares in our enterprises, caring what happens to us. Is any thought more consoling? What are we human beings that God should care for us? How can it happen that God should regard us as the apple of her eye?

These are deep matters, ultimate mysteries, driving to the roots of what it means to be human. If we derive from the providential will of a God all-powerful and all-good, then our lives may make great sense, despite their apparent chaos. If God holds our hand, then even though we walk through the valley of the shadow of darkness, we may fear no evil.

On the other hand, if we ourselves are the sources of "God," because "God" is only an idea that we project from the depths of what we wish were the case, then our psalms (and our churches and theologies and hopes for heaven) are little different from our works of art and cosmologies. They are fictions, more or less useful, as good or bad as the degree to which they help us make it through the day, negotiate a fragile peace with the universe.

The great virtue of the genuine psalm is its honesty. The song issuing from the soul, when the soul is open to the mystery of God, is nothing pious or prefabricated. It is the music actually resounding there: the pain or joy, boredom or rapture, in fact happening. These psalms carry forth a fair measure of joy, but pain is more prominent. Now and then notes of rapture sound, but boredom is more prevalent. Almost always, however, the mere effort to address God, to sing the given psalm-tone of the day, has helped me, left me feeling better. Like regular physical exercise, it has gotten my blood flowing, loosened my muscles. Often I have begun in grouchiness, stiff and graceless, only to find that, halfway through, my mood had lifted and I felt myself drawn toward a good place.

We human beings are made to address God: sing, contemplate, pray, petition. We can only be ourselves, gain access to our full resonance, when we try to address God. A human being who does not try to address God—pray—does not love the movement of his or her spirit out toward the unlimited divine mystery, and is but half what God intended when putting the spark in our clod. There is no "humanity" worthy of the name without a passion for, a correlation with, "divinity." Individuals can describe these terms as they find best. What they cannot do, in my classroom, is separate them.

In the morning, when the question is what to make of the day, God stands before us, beckoning, inviting, welcoming. In the evening, when the question is what happened during the day, God stands behind us, offering arms into which we can fall, weary and defeated. Certainly, God also moves with us through the day, fighting the noonday devil. But the archetypal moments for dealing with God, singing psalms, are the first rays of morning and the tailings of midnight.

We come from God and we return to God. God is the darkness whence and the darkness whither. God is light, yes, in all probability too bright for our minds. God is love, we hope, purifying and forgiving. But often, the saints tell us, God is dark, leading us where we do not want to go. Can God also be, as the prophets insist, caring more for mercy than sacrifice? Can God also regard us as the parables of Jesus suggest, be eager to welcome the prodigal home? Why not? God can be whatever God wishes, anything not contradictory or evil. Above all, I hope, God is the One to whom we can pray, as the prophets and Jesus illustrate.

We can pray to God when there is no one else, and we can pray to God when there is a crowd. We can pray to God when we want to share an unearthly joy, but also when if we do not pray our hearts may break from sorrow. God knows what it is to be weary, tired down into our bones. And God knows what it is to be in love, aware of the reason we have being.

We can sing psalms to God in any of these times, these moods, these needs. The wiser we are, the more consistently we shall capitalize on this fact. So sing God a new song, if you feel one rising in your heart. Or sing God an old song, if you hear one echoing through your memory. Only do not close your mind to God, or shut down your heart. As long as you keep suffering the burden of God, keep living in the face of God's mystery, you are still a human being—an image of God, little less than the angels.

Trouble

These psalms come from trouble. I mean them to stand apart from a prior book, *How to Handle Trouble* (Doubleday, 1993), but they put into personal, devotional form some of the convictions exposed in that book. I wrote most of them during the fall of 1993, when my cancer (multiple myeloma) had returned, after a brief remission. Multiple myeloma is incurable. The mean time of survival, from diagnosis to death, is 30-36 months. At the time of writing these psalms, I had been living with myeloma for about 18 months. We were familiars, it and I, though not friends. I had come to expect pain in my bones, fatigue from chemotherapy, and wonder, day and night, about the ways of God.

Trouble, however, is everywhere. You can have completely healthy bones and still suffer severe pain, physical or emotional. You can face huge problems that threaten to plow you under. Though you avoid alcoholism and drugs, you can succumb to marital infidelity, or lose your job, or suffer a heart attack. Though you do your job conscientiously and say your prayers every night, you can find yourself the victim of gossip, or aching loneliness, or doubts about faith. Teenagers can be desperately unhappy, but so can old people. Women can worry themselves sick, but so can men. Trouble spares no age group, no ethnic group, no religious denomination. If it has yet to get its claws into your hide, count yourself lucky—but don't plan on your luck continuing.

For fifty years or so, I was one of the vast majority of Americans lucky enough never to have heard of multiple myeloma. Then, one April day that I shall never forget, I heard, joining the 11,600 or so other Americans who get a diagnosis of this disease each year. Why I heard, I have no idea. Put me in a police lineup and I am unremarkable. Ask my confessor about my moral standing and he too will probably say, "Unremarkable." Yet I have trouble: walking well, thinking straight, looking at my wife late at night without crying. From my troubles have come these psalms.

Instinctively, I have taxed God with my troubles. As a reflex of faith, I have assumed that what happens to me through multiple myeloma bears on my relationship with God. This reaction has been both naive, the response of a peasant, and tutored, the calculated policy of a theologian. Naively, I have felt that God ought to be involved with my illness. If God is a Father in heaven, a Mother regarding us as nursing children, God ought to know, be concerned, take my situation to heart.

This is anthropomorphic, picturing God on the model of a good human being. The Bible gives warrants for anthropomorphism, but not without reminding us that God's ways are different from our human ways—as different as the heavens are from Earth. But anthropomorphism still feels right to me. The more intimately I deal with God, the more familiarly, the "realer" God seems to become. In times of trouble I want God to seem eminently real. I want God close, to hear my railing, have no doubts about my needs.

The theologian in me, the trained academic thinker, has reached the same convictions. God is responsible for the world, in all its particulars. The universe is a system, a unified field. Secondary causes play their parts, but the basic design, and so the ultimate responsibility, resides with God. Multiple myeloma is the result of an immensely complicated network of biological and chemical interactions that stretch back in time for tens of millions of years. I did not design my genes, nor did my parents. If I am to picture the reasons, the causes, for multiple myeloma accurately, I have to recede along a chain that quickly passes out of my sight, down into the depths of cosmic history. "God" is the name I give to the rational agency responsible for that history. God is the first cause of my myeloma, as of your diabetes and our friend's striking blue eyes.

Trying to gather thoughts and feelings like these together, I sometimes picture God moving in the marrow of my bones. That is where the cancer focuses; that is the site of the mindless cloning. So I put God at a duplicating machine there, watching it produce excessive plasma cells. If God is the source of my being, and the architect of the pattern of creation within which I live, this picture is not silly, not ignorant, not self-indulgent. God is more intimate to me than I am to myself. God is the more significant cause of my marrow than I am. If you have healthy marrow, thank God. Since I have diseased marrow, I must blame God.

"Blame," of course, is tricky. Accusing God, Job learned that his right to sue was limited. Can I be sure that multiple myeloma is an evil, a bad turn God has done me? Yes and no. Yes, it is an evil, because only a fool would say that cancer—unnatural, aberrant cellular growth—is good. If I "ought" not to suffer the pain, destruction, and death that multiple myeloma implies, then my disease is evil and God's part in it puts God under a cloud.

But perhaps also no. Perhaps multiple myeloma is also not an evil. Perhaps my experience of it can do me good. Because of multiple myeloma, I may become wiser, more compassionate, more realistic than I was before I contracted it. I may end my life a more significant person than I would have if I had stayed healthy until hit by a truck.

There is no way of telling. I would be sappy to think that cancer has given my life special distinction. Equally, however, I would be stupid, and perhaps also arrogant, to insist that cancer had ruined my life, scrawled across my time a horrible *finis*. The fact is that as long as I can think, and pray, the significance of my life remains in play, in process.

Trouble forces me to grapple with huge, in many ways unpleasant questions, but it does not determine that my life become tragic. I continue to have today, these hours, as you do, and neither of us knows much about tomorrow. Sometimes I think that if any person dealt well, fully gracefully, with a single day the heavens would open, the turtledove beguile the whole land.

Trouble, then, is partly in the soul of the one who experiences it. What we make of what happens to us is as important as what occurs physically. "Cancer" is just a word. It takes on the meaning we finally attribute to it through a steady series of experiences. The drip of the chemotherapy bottle, and the battles with the walker, and the migraine headaches, and the scars from the insertion of the two-foot rod toss in their contributions. So do the flashes of worry across your friend's face, the wet nose of your wife snuggling close, the granite slab of weariness that finally makes you head for bed.

Given the chance, I would have missed this series of experiences. I would have taken a bye, passed on the option, punted, for I think that masochism is sick. But I did not have the option. Trouble came and sank its teeth into me like a Lyme tick, or a pit bull, or an angry shark—escalate the figure as you wish. And because trouble did this, giving me no option, my prayer changed considerably. I began singing different psalms, hearing different tones, needing different answers.

I hope your prayer is not dominated by woeful troubles. I do not want you or your children to be driven to this book by pain. But if you are, if right now you are holding it with an ache in your heart or a throb at your temple, I hope some of these psalms may console you.

Using This Book

You should use this book with the utmost freedom. If a given psalm, in whole or part, "works" for you, helps you out, you should make it your own—speak it out to God, chew it down into your soul. If another psalm says nothing to you, offends you, or puts you off, you should discard it like a bad onion. The rule in prayer is to follow the leading of God's Spirit in your spirit. You should linger with what catches your attention, or moves you toward peace, or lifts your spirit in joy. Analogously, you are wise to pay attention to what challenges you, or even what makes you sad. Your spirit, like your body, has places that are tender. You will learn important things by ministering to these places, noting the pains and pleasures they provide you.

No one can make your prayer for you. Any prayer book, including that of the biblical psalms, has to be adapted. Even if you wrote your own prayer book, you could not use it next year without adapting it. Prayer always comes from here and now, this cross-section of joy and sorrow. The most that any words can carry is the beginning of the gift of yourself that turning to God here and now may prompt. Packing yourself into the words, or climbing on them like winged steeds, you begin to move up and away. As you move, though, you leave behind your original ties, your tethers to earth. Your depression or diabetes or worry about a wayward child moves into the limitless silence of God, where you hope, you pray, it receives a sympathetic hearing.

The limitless silence of God, or however else we ought to picture divinity in itself, the immediate mystery, is the destination of all these psalms. My goal in writing them is not to talk to myself, compose sermons in the mirror. My goal is to catch on the wing a thought, an image, a feeling born of how it is going between God and me at the moment, our soul-deep intercourse. I believe God is interacting with me in this process. What I think, what I feel, how my soul comes to move is in part the result of God's influence. I cannot say with any precision which images come from God and which straight from my own memory. I do not know why today I have thought x when yesterday it never occurred to me. But overall, globally, my prayer rests on an assumption, a gamble, that by turning toward God, opening my mind and heart in God's "direction," I come under God's influence, become the beneficiary of God's grace.

Following a long tradition of people who have tried to discern what actions in prayer come from God, I assume that the thoughts, feelings, and images that strengthen me—help me make it through the day—are effects of God's grace. Tied into this assumption is the further one that God is on my side, wants me to survive, and even works for my prospering. Certainly, these assumptions are vulnerable. Still, without them I see no reason to pray. If prayer is not a basic and healthy mode of being human, a way of using one's mind and heart primordially good, I see no sense in pursuing it.

I am not interested in self-deception. Merely distracting myself has little appeal. Each day I find the mysteriousness of my situation, of our common human situation, both fully objective and uniquely fascinating. This mysteriousness is the most interesting thing in my life, the most intriguing aspect of our human condition. Prayer is a direct response to this mysteriousness. It lets me contemplate the one comprehensive reality that never lets me down and may, just may, give my life surpassing meaning.

Therefore, I urge you to use these psalms, and any other prayers that you may take in hand, to mediate your encounters with the divine mystery, usher you into God's own presence. Because I must use words, from the outset my psalms are condemned to fail. Words are too thick, too clumsy, too fixed to deal adequately with the divine mystery. They serve us best when we move with them until they lose their momentum and then we let them go, abiding in the silence that follows their crashing.

Do not be afraid of this silence. If the testimony of people who have prayed with special success is valid, this silence can become your great friend. It will not patronize your troubles. It will never pooh-pooh your pain. Always it will taxi round your neighborhood, keeping an eye out for whether you want to hail it. Often it will offer itself to you like a cushion, even a bosom soft and full, providing great comfort.

Life is not amenable to propositional answers. Seldom if ever will a sentence flash across your mind pointing to the promised land. Life is usually "solved" by walking, suffering, moving on. With time, we grow accustomed to the silence draped over all the great issues, the darkness prevailing as soon as we go below the superficial mind. I shall be delighted if any of my psalms make this silence or darkness congenial.

Finally, I am writing avowedly for people in

trouble. The 75 psalms presented here are not apportioned even-handedly, half for the cheerful or optimistic, and half for the melancholy. Certainly, I do not want to cast cold water on grounds, including specifically religious ones, for enthusiasm or positive thinking. But here I am more interested in pain, confusion, depression—harsh encounters with death and disease, with injustice and evil.

Whether these negative dimensions of human experience are more powerful than the positive dimensions bidding to counterbalance them, I do not know. If a given reader wanted to argue that that they are not, that where sin has abounded grace and beauty have abounded the more, I would be happy to entertain his or her arguments. The only assumption I make is that enough people have trouble, find life painful, feel forced to wonder about the benevolence of God to justify a book of prayers rooted in sorrow and tears, as this one is. Enough people eventually have their health break down, or see their friends lacerated, or think they are witnessing the triumph of the wicked over the good to require people of faith, potential psalmists, to give an accounting for this phenomenon. That is all I have tried to do.

1

O GOD, INCLINE
UNTO MY AID.

O LORD, MAKE HASTE
TO HELP ME.

O God, incline unto my aid.
O Lord, make haste to help me.
In the dead of night
I hear the furies howl.
Even in daylight I feel besieged.
Without your support, I fall down and down
as through an endless abyss.
But you, my God, can stop my falling.
When you are near, my fears vanish.
There is no health or justice outside me.
Within my sins make me blush.
If you are not Lord of the outside
mistress of my soul
I shall never find peace.
Come, then—draw near.
Do not continue to stand far off.
I have no right to call upon you
But you need not stand on rights.
You can be gracious and merciful
longsuffering and abounding
    in steadfast love.
You can be God
like to whom is no other.

2

DEAR GOD

IN THE CLARITY OF YOUR DAWN

THE DAY STRETCHES FORTH FRESHLY.

Dear God
    in the clarity of your dawn
    the day stretches forth freshly.
What is not possible with you?
Help us to believe
    throughout this day
    that grace abounds over sin
    health is greater than sickness.
You know how hard
    this belief can be for us.
You know the limits of our frame.
The rich keep gouging the poor.
Many of the clergy are feckless.
At our right hand and our left
    loved ones sicken.
If you do not protect us
    surely we shall perish.
At dawn
I see the rays of your protection spread.
You give light to our eyes
    hope to our hearts.

3

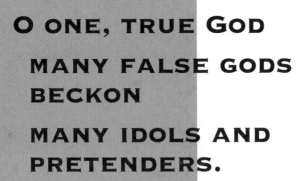

O ONE, TRUE GOD

MANY FALSE GODS
BECKON

MANY IDOLS AND
PRETENDERS.

O one, true God
   many false gods beckon
   many idols and pretenders.
In my time of trial
   they show their complete lack of worth.
None of them holds a life's weight.
All are as fragile as I am.
Unless you are real
   completely other
   my life signifies nothing.
I praise you, my God,
    for troubling me to make all this clear.
If I were not deathly ill
   my need were not fully manifest
I might continue to miss you.
But you have scored my flesh
   broken my pride
   made me see the depths
   of my nothingness.
By your grace
   in this moment of peace
   I thank you.
   my God

4

LET ALL THE PEOPLES PRAISE YOU!

LET EVERY STAR AND CLOUD CRY OUT!

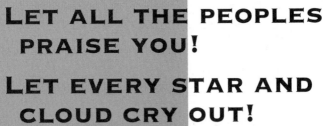

Let all the peoples praise you!
Let every star and cloud cry out!
Our troubles are tiny before you
    the smallest portion of creation.
When you let us forget our troubles
    draw us into your majesty
    our souls break out in joy
    our spirits delight in praise.
Without praise of you
    we live like moles and troglodytes
    lampreys blind to the sun.
The way out is the way in.
Cure of the soul is not talky
    no province of Narcissus.
Cure of the soul is the touch of your Breath
    the caress of your Spirit
    the Word of your love still and small.
All the best things in your world
    come as unpredictable surprises.
All the best things in your world
    are gifts, donations, grace.
If you should count iniquities
Who of us could bear it.
But you do not, O God, you do not.
Let all the peoples praise you!

5

HAVE MERCY UPON ME, O GOD,

ACCORDING TO THE ABUNDANCE OF YOUR MERCIES.

Have mercy upon me, O God,
    according to the abundance of your
    mercies.
Much in my life is untidy.
The good I have wanted to do
I have not
    and the messes I did not want to make
    I often have.
If you are a strict accountant
I shall always end up in the red.
So be more than an accountant.
Be my helper, my lover, my friend.
I need someone always on my side
    someone who will never let me down.
I need someone not like me
    someone always good, longsuffering,
    and kind.
You can be this, God.
You are not limited as we are.
You do not need flattery or fawning.
With you we can let our hearts boil over
    speak our full and honest mind.
Often, I feel lousy
    worn down or eaten up by care.
My blood is punk, my mood is sour
    there is no comeliness in me.
I cannot imagine that you like me
    that you love me seems beyond the pale.
But then I remember that you made me.
    and that you never despise the work of
    your hands.

6

HELP ME, MY GOD, FOR MY ENEMIES ARE REMORSELESS.

Help me, my God,
   for my enemies are remorseless.
From morning to night
I hear the snap of their jaws.
The world has always been sinful.
No time or place has ever lacked wrong.
But it is still bitter to find my own place cor-
roded
   sin high, low, banal right here.
Many of my friends counsel "realism."
"Expect nothing to be done well," they say.
O God, do not let me become so cynical.
Do not extinguish your spark in my clod.
It is better to be hurt than hopeless
   to seem naive than to give up on right.
It is better to feel lonely and stupid
   than to laugh in brittle despair.
Remind me how many good people keep
   trying
   stay at their posts, keep doing their jobs.
Remind me of my own failures
   all the ways I let other people down.
Draw my eyes toward your sunrise
   my ears toward your lyrical dark.
Show me again, O God of my hopes,
   that none of our follies defeats you.

7

THE LORD IS MY GURU.
I SHALL ACCEPT NO
LESSER WISDOM.

The Lord is my guru.
I shall accept no lesser wisdom.
He teaches me 'there are few answers.
She shows me that love abides.
Below feelings
    deeper than euphoria or despair
I stand as the apple of her eye.
How I want to believe this!
Help thou my unbelief.
On bad days, when pain is paramount
    my spirit barely covers the mud,
I know nothing in me is winsome
    you cherish me for no merits.
What is there between us?
How is it that I draw you?
A man, I do not try to be seductive.
A woman, I do not presume to ask you
    out.
Yet somehow you are my lover.
When all is done, only you hold my heart.
    To my amazement we share great
    passion.
Though I have no beauty or riches or
    merits
I know you sing and dance in my soul.

8

A PATCH OF BLUE
OPENS ABOVE

GOOD NEWS TO CHEER
MY SPIRITS.

A patch of blue opens above
    good news to cheer my spirits.
You bless me beyond all deserts
    recalling your prior benefits.
In my times of trouble
    I forget your prior benefits.
My memory weakens
    and I give in to despair.
How hard I find it to live
    beyond my unstable emotions.
When my bones are sore, weary,
    you seem to have vacated my world.
Your saints, O God, know better.
They delight in serving you at cost.
Remember that I am not strong as they are.
When I cannot feel you
    my courage shrinks.
This good hour, then, is a godsend.
Perhaps for another week I shall persevere.
Whether I live or die
    see you well or badly
I remain the work of your hands.
Let that be my consolation.
Not to us, O Lord, not to us
    but to your own name give glory.

9

I WATCH A GROUP OF
BEREAVED SPOUSES
STEADILY DRAW IN
THEIR HORNS.

I watch a group of bereaved spouses
   steadily draw in their horns.
It is a time for licking their wounds
   healing their traumas
    hearing their good friends wish and pray
   them well.
But the man leading the group
   raises the wall more than need be.
Spouses have no monopoly on grieving.
Almost all of us help ourselves by reaching
   out.
True, outsiders may not sense the right
   timing
   whether the harvest is yet ripe.
In your mercy, God,
   harvest all our seasons.
Make the spring and the fall
   the raw and the cooked
   flow into your plan.
What will be will be.
If I were a believer, what would bother me?

10

THE DAY STRETCHES BEFORE ME WITH NOTHING BLUNTING ITS MEANINGLESSNESS.

The day stretches before me
   with nothing blunting its meaninglessness.
All things depend on you for their meaning.
I feel this now oppressively.
Little with which we concern ourselves lasts.
Most that we accomplish is tarnished,
   imperfect.
The older we are
   the more we wish we had not seen.
Yet we have no right to be gloomy.
You have placed us in a beautiful world
   given us much more than you might have.
Against you we have no rights
   and the better we are
   the less we want them.
Your saints, O God, want only you.
How rare the air they breathe!
I keep trying to make deals:
   both prosperity now and full heaven later.
But the sand in my glass runs out.
   everything temporal loses its luster.
If I could see your face, hear your welcome,
   everything would change.

11

O GOD, OUR GOD,

YOU HAVE BEEN A
STRONG REFUGE
IN BAD TIMES PAST

O God, our God,
  you have been a strong refuge
  in bad times past
  a joy and a sun shining.
To you we can go
  whatever our problems
  however we feel.
There is no other God like you.
At the edge of our minds
  below the bottom of our spirits
  you hold all things in being.
Nothing need defeat you.
Though our hearts condemn us
  you are greater than our hearts.
Though our bodies break down
  you invite us into your deathlessness.
In your mercy,
  help us to believe in your deathlessness.
Stop our mouths from rattling
  fix our brains against foolishness.
Only you can say who you are
  what you choose to be for us.
If you wish, O God,
  you can make us well.

12

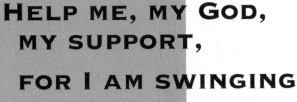

**HELP ME, MY GOD,
MY SUPPORT,
FOR I AM SWINGING
AT THE END
OF MY TETHER.**

Help me, my God, my support,
    for I am swinging at the end of my tether.
For days I have been barely enduring
I don't know how much longer I can last.
I arise most mornings discouraged
    my head heavy, my body slow.
I retire many nights crying
    wetting my pillow with shame.
Your people ought to cope better
    not toss themselves hither and yon.
I have lost most of my courage.
Every little thing gets me down.
Once I enjoyed fine prospects.
Like a meadow my life opened out.
Now my ways are dull and labored.
You have clouded my soul
    ripped my fine dreams away.
What good does this do you, O God?
How can our misfortune redound to your
    praise?
Into your hands I commit my spirit
    but my bones give me little joy.
I do not ask for money or status.
I have no desire for worldly fame.
It would be enough
    to feel your peace in my soul.

13

THOSE WHO SPEAK
DO NOT KNOW

THE TOLL THAT
SUFFERING TAKES.

Those who speak do not know
   the toll that suffering takes.
When we suffer to the marrow
   there is no comeliness in us
   and we expect to stand alone.
Now and then this brings its own comfort.
When there is nothing left to lose
   we may consider the lilies of the field
   remember everything has always been
   grace.
We may see that nothing ever matters
   because human beings think it does.
Only you can unwither the grass
   preserve the flowers from fading.
And you are so beautiful that
   sometimes my soul aches.
I hope that your beauty will always be
   apparent
   but it is enough that once it was.
What will be after my awareness of you ends
   does not matter
You need only let us adore you now
   because by your silence
   you have redeemed all our words.

14

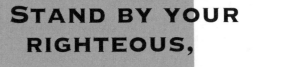

Stand by your righteous,

for we need to believe that you want justice.

Stand by your righteous,
    for we need to believe that you want
    justice.
Where have you fled
    while the good perish and the evil
    succeed?
Why have you made a world
    less perfect than our human conscience?
Why do you tempt us
    to think you are not good?
Your Spirit takes away my mind.
I have to live below reason.
Waiting, in darkness,
    I have to let you teach me your ways.
Though centuries have passed since Job
    your sages have made no progress.
We were not present at creation.
We still have no access to your plan.
You still demand our carte blanche.
What pleases you most remains our trust.
Some days, God, that is very difficult.
Some days I wish
I had never been born.
Be merciful to us all days.
Do not forget how weak is our frame.

15

**GIVE GOOD THINGS
TO YOUR PEOPLE
AND DO NOT HIDE
YOUR FACE.**

Give good things to your people
  and do not hide your face.
Why have you made us,
  if not to hear our children laugh?
You know that we cannot understand you.
Always you are above us and beyond our
  reach.
Take pity on our struggles to keep going.
Let it be enough that we do not give up.
When we consider the delicacy of our bodies
  their blood and bones and cells
  we have to think that you have made us
  lovingly
  piece by piece and for good reason.
But so much around us falls into ruin
  that you seem to let your creation come
  to grief.
O God,
  your ways are too much for us.
Suffering and evil we can never
  comprehend.
Let it be, then,
  that when we surrender to our fate
  your guardian angels catch us up
  and take us before your throne.

16

"WHERE IS HIS GOD?"
THE MOCKING AND
ENVIOUS ASK.

"Where is his God?"
　　the mocking and envious ask.
"Does he not deserve to be laid low?"
I ask you, my God,
　　to help me pay them no mind.
The farther I live from them
　　the more peaceful I feel.
It is hard enough to endure darkness
　　without having it tainted by ill will.
Between us, you and me,
　　there is usually an accommodation.
You do not leave me adrift forever.
Human beings, though, are uneasy with
　　darkness.
They want pseudo-answers—
　　reasons, they think, why this person
　　goes bankrupt
　　cancer strikes that person down.
O, God, how seldom are there simple
　　reasons.
Until your day of judgment
　　all honest people hold their tongues.
My job now is to hold on.
In your good time
　　you shall reveal
　　why x had good fortune
　　but y came to grief.

17

WE WAIT
FOR LAB REPORTS
RESPONSES TO A JOB
APPLICATION

We wait
for lab reports
responses to a job application
a great love to come out of the east
and give our lives rich meaning.
Until we learn to wait well
we think you are not coming
our lives are waste and void.
But if we want you
and lament your not being here
you are here
our simple wanting beckons you.
Often, O God,
we seem to be only wanting
raw, wholesale desire.
Nothing pleases us.
Always there is more
to hope for
long after
compact into the imagery of heaven.
You have made us for yourself
and nothing less will do.
In your kind cruelty, God,
you have opened our hearts to infinity.

18

THE KING DESIRES
YOUR BEAUTY

AS THOUGH RELIGION
WERE A MARRIAGE.

The king desires your beauty
    as though religion were a marriage.
You take what you want
    do as you have planned forever.
What are we
    that you care for us?
What standing can we have or rights?
For you to be God
    nothing can constrain you.
Your ways with us are only orderly
    when and as you choose.
And yet there are signs that you suffer.
Sometimes after midnight
    I hear you crying.
You do not want us to use our freedom
    badly.
You want love, not hatred
    mercy not sacrifice.
O God,
    you have involved yourself in our
    imperfection.
You are spotted now
    with our sin.
How long will you let this continue?
When will you come
    and wipe away every tear from your eye?

19

WE ARE IMMUNE TO MANY PATHOGENS

YET SOMETIMES OUR IMMUNE SYSTEM TURNS AGAINST US.

We are immune to many pathogens
   yet sometimes our immune system turns
   against us.
We have minds with which to discern you
   yet sometimes we think ourselves into
   trouble.
You have made us to function well
   and usually we manage
   but now and then we malfunction
   undergo seizure or cancer or sin.
The wonder is that we do so well.
How do we average seventy years
   on the whole not murdering or pillaging?
What should we infer from our bodies
   the tadpoles in the lily pond
   the images delighting our souls?
As we barrel toward death
   a straight shot to oblivion
   what ought our song to be?
You were good to give light to our eyes.
No pain or frustration wipes that out.
Naked we came into the world
   and naked we leave
   but sometimes we dress like kings
   for sometimes you touch us with love.

20

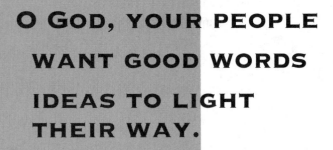

O GOD, YOUR PEOPLE
WANT GOOD WORDS
IDEAS TO LIGHT
THEIR WAY.

O God, your people
   want good words
   ideas to light their way.
You owe us prophets and teachers.
In the sadness and quiet of my trouble,
   though,
   even hallowed words empty out.
You haunt me as a steady silence
   speak by refusing to say.
I want to sink down into you
   let go and forget all words.
The whirl of my mind would drive me
   crazy.
Stop it and give me rest.
There is no answer to our worst anguish
   which is how we finally are.
We die, we don't know, we sin.
We cannot escape our selves.
You have to be our salvation.
You have to take us to heart.

21

**BAD NEWS
COMES FROM YOU
AS SURELY AS
GOOD NEWS.**

Bad news comes from you
   as surely as good news.
Man born of woman and set for the grave
   gets all his news from your plan.
Your ways grow no clearer as we age.
Though I sicken and lose my grip
   care less about things all the time
   I still understand nothing
   and hate making others worry.
That too will pass
   but how I must leave to you.
To those I love
   I cannot add a cubit's height
   subtract a liter of misfortune.
I have only today
   no certainty of tomorrow.
So if today I hear your voice
   I should treat it as a last call.
Into your obscurity
I commend my body, my spirit,
   all whom I love.

22

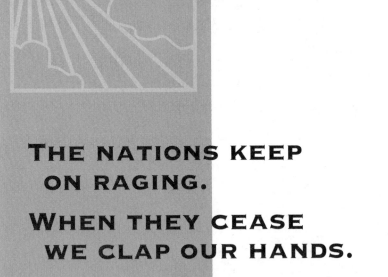

THE NATIONS KEEP
ON RAGING.

WHEN THEY CEASE
WE CLAP OUR HANDS.

The nations keep on raging.
When they cease we clap our hands.
We reward them for acting human
   not killing for a year or two.
My God, my God,
   what must you think of us?
How do we look
   from your detached balcony?
A few of us live in luxury
   while a great many starve.
In countless lands we reproduce ourselves
   mindlessly.
The main motif of our history is war.
We pay our poets and scientists little.
Once we were rich in prophets
   burning, angry men.
Once we hungered for your holiness
   loved your desert sand.
Give us back days like that,
   O God of our passionate youth.
Ignite our spirits again
   fan hate for our mediocrity.

23

**MANY OF YOUR PEOPLE
ARE BROKEN.**

**CHILDREN STARVE
CITIES BLOW APART
IN WAR**

Many of your people are broken.
Children starve
  cities blow apart in war
  AIDS reaches epidemic proportions.
The oceans remain beautiful
  and purple sunsets calm our spirits
  but hordes of us limp unhappily
  wounds in our psyches oozing.
We need healing
  and even more the assurance of your love.
We can accept the cruelties
  if we know that you are with us.
Without you,
  why should we keep going?
One day our children will be grown.
Only those who have not suffered
  whom illness has yet to score
  speak blithely of the good life.
Sometimes I want to smash them
  give them some pain to ponder.

24

WE HAVE CHOICES
TO MAKE

ABOUT HOW WE THINK
OF YOU.

We have choices to make
  about how we think of you.
If we wish
  we can make you Lord of all times
  let no pain or failure take you away.
If we wish
  we can give you carte blanche
  let you do with us what you will.
Help us to do this
  think of you this way
  redeem all times
  good and bad
  by giving you carte blanche.
Then all times and seasons are yours
  yours all feelings and moods
  today and tomorrow and all days
  until you call us home.

25

Two days ago
you took away
our friend

A doctor who had
cared for us well.

Two days ago you took away our friend
   a doctor who had cared for us well.
   Seven years he and his family suffered
   anxiety, pain, diminishment.
It makes no sense
   like so many other things in your world.
If we are to survive and not go crazy
   we have to stop trying to understand.
Naked we came into the world.
Bruised and battered we leave it.
What are we here for?
What do you want?
How can we best endure?
At our ending we know no more
   than when we crossed the birth canal.
The best we can do is surrender ourselves
   to the necessity dyed into our blood.
The only peace with a chance to last
   lets be what you choose to make happen.
Eternal rest grant unto our friend,
   and comfort to his heartbroken family.

26

THERE ARE GREAT DEEDS
ON YOUR RECORD

MERCIES AND FAVORS
WONDERFUL TO RECALL.

There are great deeds on your record
   mercies and favors wonderful to recall.
Often I forget them
   all the graces of days gone by.
You have cared for me from my beginning
   taught me to love your name.
I have not been one of the Gentiles
   wandering with no sense of your law.
I should recall this blessing regularly
   pore over your promises again and again.
I should renew my faith in your providence
   my own resurrection
   life without end in your courts.
   I cannot judge you by my standards.
The world itself has no measure for you.
I must let you be your own proofing
   let you make sense of time as you choose.
Until I come into your presence
   I have no capacity to judge what you
   have done.
So give me a spirit of endurance
   trust that you are just.

27

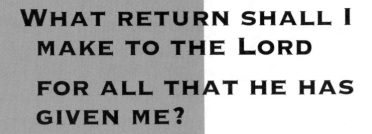

WHAT RETURN SHALL I MAKE TO THE LORD FOR ALL THAT HE HAS GIVEN ME?

What return shall I make to the Lord
   for all that he has given me?
What riches have I on which to draw?
I have no riches
   no merits
   nothing to make me interesting.
I come before you
   naked of virtue and accomplishment.
I have only my sufferings
   quite commonplace:
   the ruin of my body
   the whining of my spirit
   the zig-zagging of my rabbit mind.
These are ordinary crackups
   popular, predictable, even vulgar
   but I can anoint them
   with my yes.
I can say
   so be it
   glad to let myself go.

28

AS THE SUN WORKS
OFF THE FOG

RESTORING OUR VISION
OF THE LAND

YOUR SPIRIT WORKS

As the sun works off the fog
　　restoring our vision of the land
　　your Spirit works in our souls
　　overcoming the miasma of sin.
So often we lose perspective
　　no longer feel you can be in charge.
You are too subtle for us
　　our faith is too weak to keep you real.
In yourself, though,
　　reason says,
　　you are fully real
　　the source of all creation.
Be this for us emotionally.
Help us to feel
　　that though all things pass
　　you remain
　　our absolute foundation.

29

O GOD,

REMEMBER THE WIDOW
AND ORPHAN

THE STREET PEOPLE
AND DRINKERS

O God,
   remember the widow and orphan
   the street people and drinkers
   the old person afraid late at night.
From your divine mercy look out and see
   all the unprotected
   those with no schooling
   no churching
   no medical care.
Too easily do we in the middle classes
   grow judgmental and hard
   forgetting that you shall judge us
   as we judge your poor.
So much is good fortune
   not our achievement
   due more to genes than hard work
   or virtue.
Blessed are the poor in spirit
   who identify with your little ones
   stand up for the defenseless
   resist the strong gougers.
Blessed are the pure in heart
   who live against all the worldlings
   have here no lasting city
   because you have given them
   a glimpse of your throne.

30

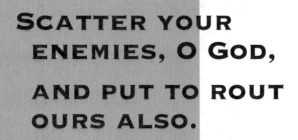

SCATTER YOUR ENEMIES, O GOD, AND PUT TO ROUT OURS ALSO.

Scatter your enemies, O God,
   and put to rout ours also.
Push back warfare and famine
   floodtide and earthquake
   tuberculosis and cancer and all other
   scourges.
Stand by the poor
   soften the rich
   to push forward justice, mercy, and
   compassion.
Hate, O God, our ungodliness
   our scoffing at beauty
   despising of conscience
   loud braying folly that belittles religion.
Remember how fear shrinks people's hearts
   leaving us small
   unwilling to try.
But also encourage the large-hearted
   the strong and courageous
   the singers of psalms to your beauty and
   might.
Be our great champion
   our leader and ruler
   the best of all gods
   that ever have been.

31

BE YOU YOURSELF OUR
INMOST TEACHER

DISCERNER OF SPIRITS

RABBI, PRIEST, PIR.

Be you yourself our inmost teacher
   discerner of spirits
   rabbi, priest, pir.
With you,
   we can do all things,
   bear all things
   expect a new heaven
   hope for a new Earth.
Without you we can do nothing.
In your Spirit, O God,
   we would not seek you
   if you had not branded your name in
   our soul.
And we do seek you
   long to behold your face.
We do want you
   like the lover of lovers
   the friend of friends
   the singular beauty
   that takes breath itself away.

32

YOU COME TO US WHEN WE ARE BROKEN

DEPRESSED AND DISCOURAGED

You come to us when we are broken
　　depressed and discouraged
　　helping us handle very bad news.
You give us your Spirit
　　to lift our low spirits
　　move us out from the dead ends we fear.
And for us you are not the brute being
　　the power of powers
　　you were for our people
　　in earlier times.
You are meaning, possibility, the end of the
　　tunnel
　　the new chance the old ending offers
　　right now.
Are you this through death also?
Can you be this through death?
Can you make of our dying
　　a new mode of living
　　a resurrection to another dimension
　　where the old limits and pains
　　fall clean away?
I cannot say yes for certain
　　but who can say no for sure?
I can say maybe, at least maybe
　　and now saying that cheers me
　　raises my forehead,
　　smooths away my beetlebrow.
I can say could be
　　would be fully fitting
　　　joins with the goodness "God" ought to
　　　imply.

33

I IMAGINE MY WAY FORWARD

(A DANGEROUS BUSINESS)

I imagine my way forward
    (a dangerous business)
    to the days when the new medicines
    take hold.
I think of the burden my body may become
    the fugues likely to take away my mind
    and I weep.
Not so much for the pain or trial
    as for the waste
    the ruin that sums up
    our bare human plight.
We always die
    and often we are not happy.
The most beautiful of our fruits
    soon goes to rot.
The best grace of our children
    can vanish overnight
    crashing in a destruction of soul.
Keep us
    from discouragement.
Let the evil of any given day suffice.
I do not have to manage next week's
    troubles.
From this sunrise to sunset is more than
    enough.

34

YOU STAND APART
SILENT

WAITING FOR US
TO TURN TO YOU

You stand apart silent
    waiting for us to turn to you
    hoping that we shall not always be stupid
    wanting that beginning of wisdom
    so long called fear of the Lord.
Right fear of you is not craven
    bending our backs
    rubbing our noses in ashes and dust.
Right fear is plain realism
    the spread of the planets
    mitochondria interferon particles of
    plasma.
You are there, God, over-against us
    immovable as the mystery we never
    escape.
You are here, God,
    more central than our cerebellum
    making us who we are
    more than we do ourselves.
And, I believe,
    you are listening and speaking,
    observing and caring—
    being here alive
    full of laser consciousness.
I cannot prove this
    and I'm not sure I want to
    but I can believe it
    if only because I have to
    if only because otherwise
    I would shriek in the night.

35

YOUR PEOPLE WANT
TO PRAY TO YOU

BUT OFTEN
OUR TONGUES THICKEN

Your people want to pray to you
    but often our tongues thicken
    our minds grow mute.
    We do not know where to begin
    how to tell you
    either our need
    or our love
    burning like acid.
We love you, God,
    the way our blood pumps
    our skin registers the breeze
    the circling hawk draws with pleasure
    our eye.
You are in us so deeply
    our desire and definition
    that no words touch your substance
    or remove it from our own.
So did your prophets become babblers
    and your darkness shut down your
    mystics' minds.
So do you still dwell in a cloud
    overshadowing our reason
    filling our hearts
    quickening our souls.
Not even our pain hands you over simply
    beyond cavil or counting
    but in bad times it is enough
    to feel that you hold us.

36

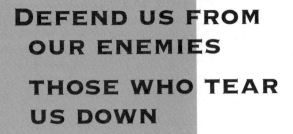

**DEFEND US FROM
OUR ENEMIES
THOSE WHO TEAR
US DOWN**

Defend us from our enemies
   those who tear us down
   are glad that we've tumbled into trouble.
Keep malice from our own hearts
   lest it eat us up
   make us ugly and alien in your sight.
We ought to treat one another well
   as brothers and sisters
   friends and friends.
Life is hard enough
   without having to battle foes within
   one's gates
   opposition around one's own campfire.
Why do we lose perspective so easily?
Why do small slights, feelings of envy,
   cause so much mischief?
When we pray well
   human status and reputation shrink to a
   laugh.
Remind us of these base lines
   in all times of trouble
   God of our living and
   God of our death.

37

HELP US BE PEACEFUL.
SUPPORT US
AS WE GO FORWARD

Help us be peaceful.
Support us as we go forward
    through sickness and conflict, much
    pain and doubt.
Life is harder than I thought it would be
    more painful, disappointing.
You do not protect us from pain.
    In the dark hours
    we think you have absented yourself
    forgotten your old fine promises.
We want to surrender ourselves
    but often we are afraid.
Place our hands together.
Set a hoop through our hearts.
Double our strength
    that we may endure for only you.

38

THE PEOPLES PLAY
AT THEIR GAMES

FOR THE MOMENT
FORGETTING
THEIR WORRIES.

The peoples play at their games
    for the moment forgetting their worries.
Like a parent watching small children
    you smile with soft, gentle eyes.
Tomorrow the peoples will return to work.
Work and play
    weekday and sabbath
    mold us in your image.
How different in you are rest and
    supervision?
What in you is labor
    contrasted with play?
Do these distinctions carry?
Is heaven good labor
    or only full rest?
The universe does immense work.
You may fling the stars out effortlessly
    but the throw itself is astonishing.
And, at the end,
    you are without measure
    not letting us know how to think of you
    lay on brainy hands
    grasp the pure mechanisms
    of elementary power and light.
You are tota simul: everythingallatonce.
We are always piecemeal.
Glory to you, only you!

39

IS IT WRONG
TO LONG FOR DEATH?
YOU GIVE US LIFE AND
TELL US TO CHERISH IT.

Is it wrong to long for death?
You give us life
  and tell us to cherish it.
The will to live
  is like the print of your thumb on our
  soul.
But we grow weary of suffering
  this pain and that
  physical or emotional or spiritual.
In later life when we examine our conscience
  we see mainly scars.
Here is the lesion from the first marriage.
See how the mark of the lost job is still red.
And more and more clearly we know
  that we don't know
  that you are not to be known
  that we shall never know you
  and that until we do know you
  all else is uncertain.
There is only you
  existing independently
  not begging your significance from others.
Can we not then quit this half-life
  this recovery ward
  this asylum and mortuary?
When will you let us go home?

40

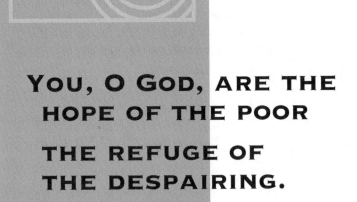

YOU, O GOD, ARE THE
HOPE OF THE POOR

THE REFUGE OF
THE DESPAIRING.

You, O God, are the hope of the poor
  the refuge of the despairing.
When all else fails
  you remain
  waiting for us to return.
You are before all other helps
  and what none of them can do
  you may be able to.
With you there is always hope
  though usually also silence.
We never control you
  so always the band plays on.
Thus do you force us to the bare truth:
  we do not run the world.
How the world runs
  where it is going
  in what way our lives will end—
  none of this do we ever know.
So give us your good Spirit
  to keep us close to you.
Help us to see and feel
  the benefits of your mysteriousness.
The world would be even more terrible
  than it is
  if we were running it.

41

WHO ARE WE, GOD, THAT YOU ALLOW US TO HOPE FOR ETERNAL LIFE?

Who are we, God,
    that you allow us to hope for eternal life?
Can we rely on the mind-bending symbols
    that promise service after death in your
    courts?
This symbolism obliges
    many Jews, all Christians,
    and all Muslims.
You live beyond time
    and those who keep faith with you in time
    move into your beyond.
Help me, dear God, to believe this
    and feel the full force of its freedom.
With you is everything for which we hunger
    beauty and goodness unbound.
The chorus of 144,000
    the tribes doubled and doubled again
    have nothing better to do
    than sing lustily your praises
    harmonizing higher and higher
    boosted by the angels and seraphim.
The center of our souls
    is made for pure worship.
If we were with you fully
    our delight would be songs of your praise.

42

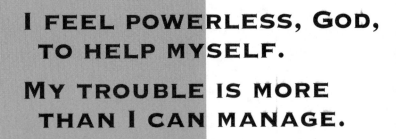

I FEEL POWERLESS, GOD,
TO HELP MYSELF.

MY TROUBLE IS MORE
THAN I CAN MANAGE.

I feel powerless, God,
    to help myself.
My trouble is more than I can manage.
I have lived with it so long
    that I know its every mote and wrinkle.
But I cannot make it go away.
It leans over me in the morning
    blocking out the sun.
It mocks me at midnight
    driving sleep away.
I do not want to be my trouble.
I resent its defining me
    pushing me to the margins of my own
    life.
Will you not give me a new definition?
Will you not be my center
    and reset all my margins?
You must be greater than my trouble
    or you are not God.
You must reduce it to the insignificance of
    an idol
    an ugly thing of wood, clay, and sin.
I want to leave it far behind me
    and travel outside myself to you.
Help me, O God, in this want
    for it quickens your life in my soul.

43

GIVE GLORY TO THE KING OF AGES

AND RECALL ALL THE DAYS OF FEASTING

Give glory to the King of Ages
   and recall all the days of feasting past.
From the dawn of human awareness,
   your people have sung songs to you.
Fear of you is the beginning of our wisdom.
Love of your light is the dawn of our faith.
But you slip through our fingers like water
   no net fine enough to hold your name.
There is none like you in the heavens
   on the seas
   under the ground
   in the music of even the best of our bards.
You are God
   dwelling apart in unapproachable light.
The darkness is your raiment
   and you strip your prophets of pretense.
We can begin our journey anywhere
   but always it ends in unknowing.
We can believe you are a good God and
   love our kind
   but we cannot guarantee it.
Only you can supply your grace.
Only God can speak for God.
So remind us of your words of old.
With your still small voice
   tell us again that you love us.

44

**OUT OF THE TURMOIL
OF MY TROUBLE**

**I SEND MY CRY
UP TO YOU.**

Out of the turmoil of my trouble
  I send my cry up to you.
Who else can understand me?
I don't understand myself.
I know that my pain is growing
  the periods of relief are becoming
  smaller.
I know that you want me to consider my end
  and prepare my soul to see your face.
May I ask, O God, one favor?
Will you limit the upset I cause?
The worst of my pain is the fear I see
  in the eyes of those who love me.
There is little they can do for me
  which bothers them greatly.
The better friends they have been
  the more thoughts of me oppress them
  and so the more guilty they feel.
You have connected us more sensitively
  than the most sophisticated
  telecommunications.
The fear of one stirs the fear of many others
  so we must all try to stay strong.
I have now done most of what I shall have.
My summing up is well under way
Look not, O God, on our accomplishments
  but on the delight you felt
  when first you made us be.

45

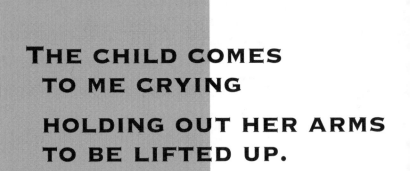

THE CHILD COMES
TO ME CRYING

HOLDING OUT HER ARMS
TO BE LIFTED UP.

The child comes to me crying
　　holding out her arms to be lifted up.
How often I come to you that way
　　though I don't even realize it.
I feel like an orphan out on my own
　　dirty, ashamed, alone.
This little girl has been beaten up.
　　she feels broken, rejected, abused.
O God, God,
　　is there no end to your people's suffering?
The pain goes down and down and down
　　circling like a bottomless pit.
I tell the child she need not be heroic.
Getting through the day is victory enough.
I speak to her
　　but I listen for myself—
　　I have yet to learn that lesson.
None of us has surety of this time tomorrow.
Each of us can only find you, serve you,
　　right now.
Help us to feel,
　　O God of the abject, Lord of the outcast,
　　that even our wretchedness has some use.

46

DO NOT TURN ASIDE
FROM US, O GOD,

NOW THAT WE CALL
TO YOU IN NEED.

Do not turn aside from us, O God,
   now that we call to you in need.
Do not hide your face forever
   while we languish without comfort.
You have made us to seek your face
   and to ask for your help.
You have made us to find here on Earth
   no lasting city.
So you must yourself be our city
   the place where we love to dwell.
And you must yourself be our refuge
   our shade in the heat of day
   our breeze in the cool of evening.
There can be for us none but you.
Without you we lack our reason to be.
The best of friends cannot sustain us.
The worst of enemies cannot ruin us.
No matter what the circumstance
   you are our crux.
In both good times and bad
   you are our measure and meaning.
Be merciful to us, then,
   and respect what you have made.
Take us from our depths into yourself—
   your love from time out of mind.
Make it right that for us there is you alone.

47

I WANT TO LIVE.
DO NOT TAKE MY LIFE
AWAY EARLY.

I want to live.
Do not take my life away early.
Set me with you
   in the midst of your deathlessness.
Lead me kindly into your light.
You are the Lord of my flesh
   and the God of my tattered spirit.
You number my days one by one
   like knots on an Incan string.
My story will end when you choose
   in the way and pattern of your desiring.
The world itself will continue or end
   by counsels you share only with wisdom.
You want me to want to live—
   the very pain in my bones tells me so.
I would not hate it
   would not care enough to fight it
   would not want the tumors out
   had you not made me for life and health
   were you not a God in love with the
   living.
But where I should live
   how I should find you
   what my consummation ought to be—
   all that I must commend to your keeping.

48

**WE TRY, O GOD,
TO KEEP GOING.**

**WE LOOK FOR REASONS
TO PERSEVERE.**

We try, O God, to keep going.
We look for reasons to persevere.
But our food has no taste
    we sleep badly most nights
    and who knows if our work makes a
    difference?
Vanity of vanities and all is—what?
What is the sum of this game you are
    playing?
Perhaps these are bad questions
    impertinent and disrespectful.
Perhaps ours is not to reason why
    only to do the best we can.
Many of your people are weary.
History looks like one forced march.
Few of your people now seem holy or
    happy.
Our hopes have narrowed to survival.
We are as you have made us.
If we are not impressive
    you must share the blame.
Give us, O God, causes for joy.
Gladden our hearts
    and let us see your beauty everywhere.
When we catch a glimpse of your splendor
    it is easy to keep going.
When your Spirit blows through our spirits
    we feel clean enough to continue
    and clap our hands in applause.

49

AFTER ANOTHER DAY OF BATTERING I SLUMP ON MY STOOL

After another day of battering
   I slump on my stool
   feeling black, blue, and green
   from the crashing indifference.
A few welcome surprises
   keep the fight interesting
   but several people to whom I looked for
   support
   have yet to put in an appearance.
What more can I do,
   what else display before them?
Is it not enough that I am dying?
What drama would be further?
We are a slow race
   a stupid species
   beguiled by baubles and dreck.
Probably I should just pray that you forgive
   them
   as you forgive me
   because neither of us knows what we do.
What we do is keep bumbling forward
   little more reflective than monkeys.
What we do is salve our consciences
   hone our distractions
   rationalize the self-centered ways that
   we live.
In the end, we flee from ourselves
   lest your Spirit grab us by the neck
   and twist us around to live.

50

WHAT SHOULD WE HOPE TO ACCOMPLISH

WITH THE TIME THAT YOU GIVE US?

What should we hope to accomplish
    with the time that you give us?
How can we generalize
    about a successful life pleasing to you?
Let our lives, O God,
    project praise of your goodness
    gratitude for the world's beauty
    and thanksgiving for the love of our
    friends.
Let them also express dedication
    to the improvement of other people's
    welfare.
May it be clear that we have tried
    to help the poor
    comfort the sick
    enlighten the ignorant.
O God, often what we do
    seems to make little difference.
The inertia of our economy grinds along.
The baleful patterns of race, class, and sex
    shape generation after generation.
Break the patterns that you find vicious.
Call forth new leaders
    with fresh energy and ideas.
Remind us that there are changes we can
    make
    differences and innovations.
Help us to believe that the future can be
    bright
    because with you a new creation is
    always possible.

51

THE SEAS RUSH IN
FURIOUSLY

THREATENING TO
OVERWHELM US.

The seas rush in furiously
  threatening to overwhelm us.
Our lives bob and rise like corks.
We feel terribly vulnerable, God.
If woe does not come today
  we have to fear it tomorrow.
Surely the answer is to abandon ourselves
  letting you work for us what you will.
Living or dying we can be yours
  if we want only what you do.
But what do you want, dear God?
Seldom is your will fully clear.
After the fact we can say that you chose our
    success
    or our sickness, or our death
    but before and during these experiences
    little about them is clear.
I am tired of struggling to understand your
    ways
    weary of searching for your will.
Let your Spirit lift me to where you want
    me to be.
Be yourself the prime agent of my obedience.
I wish my service were more distinguished
  but I cannot give you what I do not have.
The poverty of what I can offer you
  will have to be most of my gift.
Let me be remarkable for the tatters of my
    uniform
    the worn jacket and knock-about shoes.

52

THE PEOPLE WRINKLE
WITH WORRY.

CONCERN BENDS
THEIR SHOULDERS

The people wrinkle with worry.
Concern bends their shoulders
    shrinks their souls.
Anxiety about money and health wear
    them down.
They cannot let the morrow alone
    the future take care of itself.
Consider the lilies of the field, O God,
    laid before us as our model.
Consider the carelessness of natural
    creation
    which seldom has to worry.
Could you not let us feel your presence
    like a breeze across our brow
    energy surging in our blood
    to make us similarly careless?
Could you not help us face death
    once and for all
    and so step out of our regular nightmare?
When we know why we are suffering
    we carry on more bravely.
If there is a reason for our cross
    it feels more redemptive.
But the great reasons are lost to our sight.
We do not see the proportions of your plan.
What you are building through time
    is too vast for us to manage.
Hold our hand.

53

DAY FOLLOWS DAY
JUST AS THE OLD
AUTHORS DESCRIBED IT.

Day follows day
   just as the old authors described it.
If there is anything new under the sun
   it has little to do with pain.
Sometimes I think the best tactic
   is to keep one's hand on today
   like a guard checking an opponent
   lest he feint and swoop to the hoop.
We can try to stay in touch with your
   mysteries
   your depth shimmering down out of
   sight.
We can ask you to be good to those we love
   and remember the weakness of our
   carriage.
But any day you can move in to crush us
   overturn our lives in a flash.
To be human is to be vulnerable
   live with one's throat to the knife.
O God, you can also be kindly.
You need not try us forever.
With you there can be comfort and
   consolation.
Remember that, God, this day.
Give us good things to celebrate
   reasons for praising your name.
We want to worship you faithfully
   but we are weary and hard-pressed.
So carry us like tired children.
Wash us and dress our wounds.

54

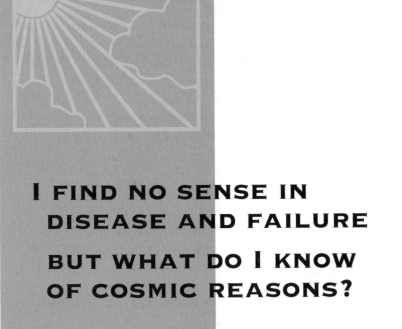

I FIND NO SENSE IN
DISEASE AND FAILURE

BUT WHAT DO I KNOW
OF COSMIC REASONS?

I find no sense in disease and failure
  but what do I know of cosmic reasons?
O God, you do much statistically.
So many people get cancer of type x each
  year.
Their mean time of survival is y number of
  months.
In their cells, proteins and other components
  interact somewhat predictably.
They are animals
  composed as animal life is
  operating as animal life does.
Few of us get any exemption from our
  animality.
Most of us follow the rules, are not the
  exceptions.
Why do the rules drive us toward death?
Why do some sicken young
  feel the hot breath of breakup
  prematurely?
You keep the answers to yourself.
The evil in the world is your private secret
  we hope not dirty and little.
We did not make the world
  witness the creation
  so we have no standing for suing.
We can only ask that you remember
  your own better nature.
Be a God of life and love.
Stand by us in our suffering
  wipe away all our tears.

55

IF I AM YOUR CHILD, PERHAPS I ALSO AM DEATHLESS

If I am your child,
  perhaps I also am deathless
  taken up into your life, beyond decay.
Only you know the truths of this.
I must sicken in faith.
But the biblical covenants that I treasure
  the canonical symbols of our relations
  make sharing life all-important.
You share our lives—
  through your interest
  the movements of your Spirit in our
  hearts
  your ongoing grant of existence
  the enfleshment of your word.
You happen to us
  pitch your tent in our midst
  overcome the great nought at our center.
Do you also share your life?
Does your undying divinity
  reach to the fine points of our spirit
  draw us into your eternity
  make us so one with you that what you
  are we are
  that your heaven becomes our Earth?
"The life of the world to come"
  is an article of the biblical creeds.
The life of the world to come
  is your knowing and loving as God.

56

I THANK YOU, GOD,
FOR SMALL FAVORS.

I thank you, God, for small favors.
The new chemotherapy has begun well.
Though lethal, the drugs flooding my blood
    are giving me energy.
I smile remembering the ways of your Spirit.
Typically she coddles us in the beginning
    giving us prayer easy and sweet.
Then she withdraws her sugared breast
    weaning us to adulthood.
After this intake of drugs
    there will be the crash of withdrawal.
In the past it's been nearly audible
    a splat from 10,000 feet.
So, seizing the day, I have been indulging
    myself
    delighting in this temporary energy.
I have also been preparing
    remembering, God, the rules about
    consolation.
In times of prosperity
    we should remember desolation.
In times of desolation
    we should stir up our hopes that you
    will return.
When I have no head
    not a pious thought in my entire system
    I must keep groping through the rubble
    to hand myself over like a derelict
    a blank check scrawled in torn flesh.

57

I AM CARING LESS
FOR MY LIFE;

LET ME NOT CARE LESS
FOR THE LIVES
OF OTHERS.

I am caring less for my life;
    let me not care less for the lives of others.
My life, breaking down, more and more
    mottled,
    is detaching itself from me.
Whatever I am essentially, in soul,
    is ungluing itself from my rotting bones.
Many times I feel careless
    as though not much matters.
What will happen will happen
    when and as you choose
    and, I hope, with you in the midst of it.
But if my life matters less and less
    the venture of life itself
    the great cosmic and historical drama
    ought to matter to me more and more.
Until the day of your final coming
    it is the single great imperative.
For us not to keep faith with your creation
    to fail our stewardship over Earth
    is the one unforgivable sin.
How can we claim to love the God we
    cannot see
    when we do not love the brothers and
    sisters
    the air, the seas, the plants and animals
    that we can see?
Our religion is highly suspect
    if we do not love your Earth well.

58

I REMEMBER, O GOD, THE APATHEIA OF THE DESERT FATHERS

I remember, O God, the *apatheia* of the
    desert fathers.
It was a detachment rooted in you.
It did not oppose the world so much as the
    self—the unruliness of human desire.
Sometimes that apathy seems close
    to a blessed peace
    surpassing all understanding.
The world, the flesh, and the devil
    do not know it, do not want it.
Only those whom you take to yourself
    for whom you become so sufficient
    know it and rest in it gladly.
Grant us this peace, O God.
Grant us a proper detachment and
    complacency.
When we rest in you
    we see the world aright
    all creation come into balance.
When we struggle and strive wrongly
    all relations jangle and jar
    creation itself can seem ugly.
This day, O God, it is easy to surrender.
Tomorrow it may be hard.
Easy or hard, let me do it
    have your Spirit carry me, all your
    people, into your peace.
At the source of our being
    the ground of our hope
    the life we may gain through dying well
    you are enough.

59

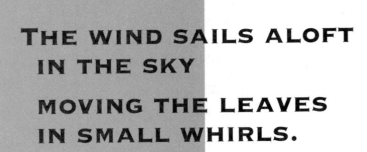

THE WIND SAILS ALOFT
IN THE SKY

MOVING THE LEAVES
IN SMALL WHIRLS.

The wind sails aloft in the sky
   moving the leaves in small whirls.
   Your Spirit calls to a little dust-devil:
"Come up higher."
Circles on circles, helixes on helixes.
Always there is more, another spiral of
   beyond.
I love your beyond, which is our freedom.
We can keep going into you, higher and
   deeper
   on and on because you have no end.
And so we have no end.
We can move farther into your light
   into the darkness of your love
   consciously, with complete delight
   but ultimately we shall continue
   however you wish
   at least as a memory that always has to be
   at least as an occasion, a moment,
   that always will have been necessary
   a dot essential to just this universe.
But your beyond may also be your intimate
   self
   the quasi-sexual center of your constant
   fertility.
We may be going to the womb of your love
   the endless goodness much greater than
   all nothingness
   the grace completely dominating all evil.
The metaphor the dust-devils can create
   is mysterious wonderfully.

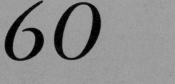

60

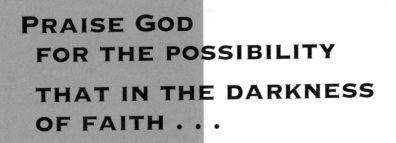

**PRAISE GOD
FOR THE POSSIBILITY
THAT IN THE DARKNESS
OF FAITH . . .**

Praise God for the possibility
    that in the darkness of faith
    the glory of divinity may be all around us
    the entirety of life and creation
    just a cloud hiding the splendor and light
    of heaven and God's own life.
That seems a crazy possibility
    until we read your saints.
From the love you pour forth in their hearts
    they become convinced that everything
    is grace.
Julian and Elizabeth and Ruysbroek
    the author of The Cloud and John of the
    Cross
    join mystics from other traditions
    to challenge the sensual limitations I
    impose
    my assumption that what I can feel
    defines what you can be.
You can be whatever you wish
    in me or the world
    because we belong to you.
We did not make ourselves.
We are yours to use as you see fit.
If you wish to use our suffering obscurely
    for ends we cannot grasp
    that is your simple right.
Our responsibility and right
    is only to say, "Your will be done."

61

**IN TROUBLE,
WE LONG
FOR MEANING.**

In trouble,
    we long for meaning.
If we could redeem our pain
    see some good in our breaking
    it would become more bearable.
So I think of love coming through suffering.
I think of your uniting yourself to us
    by breaking through all our resistances.
The world seems indifferent.
Without faith there is no indication you
    care.
But sometimes in my depths
    when I reach my center and rest
    you feel real
    spirit other than my spirit
    a context or whole
    keeping me from being alone.
And sometimes none of my failures matters
    for it is clear you can make all things new.
For the moment it is enough that you are
    that I am in you
    that things for which I have no words
    can be real.
Losing my head
    rational control
    a secure bodily sense of who I am
    is teaching me that love needs little reason
    only enough to keep hoping to see your
    face.

62

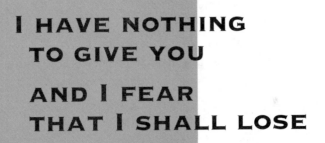

I HAVE NOTHING
TO GIVE YOU

AND I FEAR
THAT I SHALL LOSE

I have nothing to give you
 and I fear that I shall lose
 even my longing for you.
Once that longing defined my inmost self
 as in fact it defines all biblical creatures
 from Leviathan to the everlasting hills.
We want you, God.
You are the beauty driving us mad.
But we cannot find you, possess you.
You are a hidden God
 and a Lord of flies buzzing over the
 world's gore.
We wonder if our desire isn't a hoax.
Have we evolved into inevitable
 frustration—
 wanting what we can never find?
This side of death
 the best we can manage is passing
 moments of contact
 portentous but far from certain.
This side we live by darkness
 not just of mind but of will.
We have to renounce the satisfaction of
 loving you
 if you withdraw it.
We have to want you
 more than the love of you
 have to want you to be in splendor
 praised by the thrones and dominations
 more than our enjoyment of you.
Refine us in your fire.

63

HELP US TO
BE WITHOUT FUSS.

LET OUR LETTING GO
MAKE US SIMPLE.

Help us to be without fuss.
Let our letting go make us simple.
We cannot add a cubit to our height.
We shall live to the day you have appointed.
Yes, you love our yearning and creativity.
The parent in you wants us to strive.
But as we come to maturity
   you have to teach us a sterner realism:
   you are everything and we are nothing.
How do you overcome our nothingness?
What makes us come to be
   so that we can seek you
   commune with you and sink into your
   arms?
What are you?
You are love
   though saying this explains nothing.
For you to be is to be loving into being
   making something happen to share your
   warmth.
In my troubles I sink to this bottom.
It seems to hold: you are the end.
At bottom, with you, trouble loses its hold
   on me.
Who can say what a disease or a death
   finally means?
Who can be sure it does not serve a new
   life?
You, God, mean a life constantly new.
You mean an end for trouble, a limited term.
   From this end let me make a beginning.

64

LOOKING FOR A FRIEND

MY FRIEND WHO IS ALONE IN HER WORK

Looking for a friend
　　my friend who is alone in her work
　　has to keep company with her own spirit.
Some people appreciate what she is doing
　　but they are not ten in a thousand.
How much trouble is loneliness?
O God, I believe you want us to be social
　　but you have not made our sociability
　　simple.
We cannot just couple
　　or live by yea, yea and nay, nay.
Always we want to be both joined and
　　individual
　　and this wanting ripples through all our
　　troubles.
In our dying we remain individual
　　moving farther and farther away.
Strange, because we all die
　　and we all know that we all die
　　and we all sense that we could make
　　from this knowledge
　　a great vat of healing
　　if your Spirit moved us to communion
　　and we keened together over our
　　separations
　　kissed and touched and sighed
　　to the conclusion that if today we heard
　　your voice
　　we would soften our hearts with holy
　　tears
　　and feel radically equal.

65

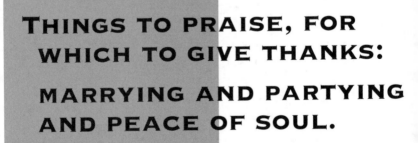

THINGS TO PRAISE, FOR WHICH TO GIVE THANKS:

MARRYING AND PARTYING AND PEACE OF SOUL.

Things to praise, for which to give thanks:
    marrying and partying and peace of soul.
You destroy me with gentleness.
    I am losing myself by being let go.
Though trouble takes hold of me
    crumpling my soul with an iron fist
    by wanting less and less
I have shrunk in the fist
    and so gained more room in which to
    maneuver.
When our troubles involve other people
    we have to stay concerned.
We must do for them what we are able
    though usually this is little.
But often we can drop our own troubles.
Often, God, we can call them your business
    and little of our own.
Yes, miracles are always flashing—
    each time a child exits from the womb.
But miracles of healing are not our doing
    probably not something we should desire.
If they would magnify your mystery
    open people's minds and hearts
    let them happen dramatically.
But usually they would not
    so normally we do best by walking
    the road that is ordinary.
Today it is quiet, thank God.

66

YOU HELP US IN OUR TROUBLES

SIMPLY BY BEING GREATER.

You help us in our troubles
    simply by being greater.
When they threaten to overwhelm us
    you remind us that you alone determine
    our worth.
If we did not die we might forget this.
If worldly life were solid we might bow to
    mammon.
Death and suffering detonate that possibility.
We have here no lasting city.
We are fools to put our trust in princes.
Health and pleasure and fame are all fleeting.
If we are not to perish as useless passions
    we must find something stable outside
    the world.
What can that be but you?
Who else never changes
    is as mysterious at our end as at our
    beginning?
O God, I love your mystery
    but I hold back from giving myself to
    you fully.
The saints abide in you continually
    having no will of their own.
Let our troubles guide us in this direction.
Strip us of false desire, impure wanting
    so that we may rejoice in whatever
    happens.
Make our prayer that your will be done
    flow from the depths of our mortality
    where we leave everything in your hands.

67

LOVELIER THAN THE BEDIZENED KINDS

AT LEAST FOR PEOPLE IN DEEP TROUBLE . . .

Lovelier than the bedizened kinds
   at least for people in deep trouble
   is a faith we can call "mere."
It sees nothing, and does not have to.
Often it feels nothing
   or the worse-than-nothing called
   desolation.
But it hangs on
   with more or less good grace
   if only because it can do no other;
   something holds it from despair.
Probing this something
   I find your utter simplicity.
There is nothing simpler than you.
The seas and the skies and the crawling
   things
   all get their forms from you.
They express your creativity
   but in itself this remains hidden
   some mysterious function of whatever
   you are at core:
   love or isness or some more ineffable
   reality.
Faith sets us in your utter primordiality.
We rest there and open our hearts.
We tell you to do with us what you will
   for that's what you will do anyway.
We ask you to show us how what you do is
   good
   and in your mercy sometimes you agree
   to.

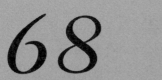

68

PRAISE GOD
FOR THE PEACE
THAT SOMETIMES VISITS

Praise God for the peace that sometimes
visits
slipping in the door unannounced!
Praise God for the joy I thought gone.
I cannot reckon with you.
You amuse yourself by sabotaging my
expectations.
When I prepared my spirit for brutal
endurance
you set a table in the presence of my
enemies
made the steroids not foes but friends.
Always I underestimate you.
Never do I come close to glimpsing your
goodness.
Give me, O God, a simpler faith.
Let me leave my reservations in the study
in the pews kneel with a peasant trust.
You know what you are doing
and you can only do it from love.
Let me cling to this abandonment like a
barnacle.
Let me not care what happens to my body
whether or not I feel you to be close.
You are the potter.
The design of my life is the impress of your
fingers.
All the passion of the lover in the Song was
for you.
Let all my passion be for you
most gracious, delicate, and trustworthy.

69

WHO HAVE THE POOR
TO HELP THEM

IF NOT YOU,
OUR UNCOOPTED GOD?

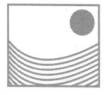

Who have the poor to help them
    if not you, our uncoopted God?
Where can we look for justice
    except to your highest heaven?
Help us, O God, to look correctly.
Do not let us flee our rightful
    responsibilities.
We should pray as though everything
    depended on us
    and act as though everything depended
    on you.
Everything does depend on us.
You will not save us against our will.
But that means that all salvation is perilous,
    for only you can save us from ourselves.
The more closely we examine ourselves
    the more passionately we shall pray.
Praying passionately, we may begin to act
    freely.
O God, such wisdom is long in coming.
Take pity on our ignorance, our reluctance
    to learn.
Why are we such strong resisters?
Why will we not embrace the things for
    our peace?
Few things are more mysterious than this
    resistance.
All our fulfillment lies in you
    yet we persist in running away.
Seduce us, O God, with your beauty.

70

THE WORLD
IS TOO MUCH WITH ME

SWIRLING MY BLOOD
AND CONFUSING ME.

The world is too much with me
   swirling my blood and confusing me.
I forget to drop out from its confusion
   do not pray to you, God, as the wholly
   other.
Yes, I believe and hope that you are always
   with me.
I love your sacramental signs.
But a hard wind should be blowing
   to keep my troubles in sharp focus.
The smog of busyness and self-
   congratulation
   is mottling my daily prayer.
Remind me, O God, that I am dying.
Do not let me lose the lessons of this disease.
What do they boil down to?
What is the gist I should recall each day?
You are my measure and meaning.
If I please you, I am successful.
If I displease you, I am botching my time.
I cannot please you without your Spirit.
You must give me the righteousness you
   require.
But I must agree to your working this out
   by watching and praying and saying
   amen to your love.
Give me an unworldly love.
Make me poor quiet unambitious, most of
   all attentive.

71

**YOU ARE A GOOD GOD
AND YOU LOVE
OUR KIND.**

You are a good God
and you love our kind.
We cling to this hope.
If you are not kindly
compassionate and merciful
longsuffering and abounding in steadfast
love
we have no good hope.
Your character determines the character of
our hope.
So help us, O God, to remember your
character.
Give us the good memory
the alert reading of times past
that underscores your provision for us
the manna in the wilderness, the quails.
Through countless generations
we have survived.
Against all odds
we have retained a remnant of believers
a little file of saints
who have not lost their way completely.
The light has kept shining in the darkness
and the darkness has not overcome it.
Show us, dear God, that this is miraculous.
Do not let us think that grace is ordinary
that faith or hope or love is ever bound
to be.

72

IF YOU YOURSELF ARE
MY SUFFERING

EVEN MY CRUCIFIXION

THE FINAL TERMS OF MY
TROUBLE COME CLEAR.

If you yourself are my suffering
    even my crucifixion
    the final terms of my trouble come clear.
What happens to me is what you desire.
You want this whole world of which I am
    part
    and you want this whole story that
    includes my life.
You do not want the accents intruded by sin.
Had I been more generous in love
    you would be beholding something better.
But you do behold me
    you are not blind
    and what you behold you love—
    you cannot hate any of the works of
    your hands.
You do not want me to suffer
    because you love me
    yet you require that I suffer
    because you love me in a world that
    entails it.
Why does my world entail suffering?
I do not know and never shall.
So I do best when I say to my suffering,
    "Come, God, my death.
    Be, pain, the touch of my Maker,
    absolutely personal between us."
Better that I disgust you or anger you
    than that you have no personal interest
    in me
    would as soon I were dark anti-matter.

73

**YOU WELCOME THE
WINDS AND SO OUR
LONGING SPIRITS.**

You welcome the winds and so our longing
   spirits.
From the abyss you watch the chipmunks
   play
   and so smile at our scatty love-lives.
In your unutterable simplicity, God,
   you can be warm, near, dear.
You are for us what you choose to be
   usually both constant and changing.
Always I can go to you
   or find you at my center.
For me to be is to be in you
   to feel is to feel toward you
   to be quiet is to flow toward your rest.
Ah, Ah, God
   it is well when I just am
   your world just is itself
   the wanting and striving slip away.
What trouble would there be
   if whatever happened brought you?
How much pain would pass away
   never grow claws
   if we began with what is
   and stuck to the core fact: only you are
   absolutely?
If we are in you now
   and can come at death to be with you
   inseparably
   how can any trouble be essential
   any upset destroy our core?

74

MY GOD, MY GOD
YOU ARE NOT
FORSAKING ME.

My God, my God
    you are not forsaking me.
Lately you have been holding me close
    laughing gently at my follies
    telling me all manner of thing will be well.
I am not used to this buoyant support.
I am more comfortable with a thin aridity.
But what I am used to or find comfortable
    is secondary.
Primary ought to be what you choose to
    give.
If you choose to give darkness
    darkness I should love.
If you give light
    light should send me dancing.
You are God
    while I am but dust and ashes.
You know this constitutionally
    and I learn it day by day.
A good person
    would handle your support simply:
"Thank you."
Sing God this simple song.
Dance it in the narthex
    belt it out in all the pews:
All my life's a circle?
What do I keep humming round?
Whatever riff or chant will please you.
Whatever death or life you choose.

75

**LATELY WHEN I TURN SAD
THINKING HOW BADLY
I HAVE SERVED YOU**

Lately when I turn sad
    thinking how badly I have served you
    how often I been full of myself
    and how many people are suffering
    how wretchedly imperfect is our world
    I feel a small tug on my heart
    see a small finger curled in beckoning.
It invites me to let go and pray.
The world ought to make any of us sad
    because the world houses much that is
    ugly and evil.
People who delight in the world uncritically
    must themselves be ugly and evil.
Yet the world is far from being our all.
You alone, God, qualify for that title.
And though you move through the world
    beautifully
    because the world is in you and you are
    in it
    you are much more than the world
    and the world plus you is no more than
    you are alone.
So, my God, I should only be sad
    if you are not enough
    or are not doing your job
    or have defaulted on your covenant.
None of these propositions is true.
You are more than enough—eternity will
    not empty you.
You are doing your job—we continue to be.
And sometimes I hear your arias.

OF RELATED INTEREST...

Healing Wounded Emotions
Overcoming Life's Hurts
Martin Padovani

Describes how one's emotional and spiritual lives interact, and challenges readers to live fuller, more satisfying lives.

ISBN: 0-89622-333-7, 128 pp, $6.95

In God's Presence
Centering Experiences for Circles and Solitudes
William Cleary

Offered are psalms, meditations, prayers and poems that will help both solitary readers and groups find a connection with God.

ISBN: 0-89622-608-5, 144 pp, $9.95

The Pummeled Heart
Finding Peace through Pain
Antoinette Bosco

The author believes that pain can be a wake-up call from God, serving to shake people out of spiritual complacency and egocentric lives.

ISBN: 0-89622-584-4, 140 pp, $7.95

Available at religious bookstores or from
TWENTY-THIRD PUBLICATIONS
P.O. Box 180 • Mystic, CT 06355
1-800-321-0411